Divorce Survival Guide For Kids

Tips To Survive Your Parents Divorce: For Kids, Written By Kids

Alexa Smith

Samantha Smith

DEDICATION

We would like to dedicate this book to our parents who worked together, setting aside their differences, to raise us and make us who we are today.

We would like to thank them for everything they do for us and how they both always support us and believe in what we do.

They taught us the true meaning of hard work and dedication, and how it's needed to get what you want. They have made so many sacrifices as single parents along the way and we truly appreciate everything they have done for us.

CONTENTS

INTRODUCTION: WHY I'M WRITING THIS BOOK

It's been twelve years since my parents first separated and got divorced. That means two-thirds of my life, or basically all of my childhood and teen life, I have been a child of a divorced family. I think that makes me an expert in dealing with divorced parents and the situations being in a divorced house brings on!

So why did I finally decide to write this book? I wanted to share with other kids the things I've learned to make being in a divorced family easier. I've always been known as the kid with divorced parents and two homes. As a result, over the last ten years, I have helped many friends when their parents were fighting and they were worried their parents were going to get divorced. They would ask for advice because they were worried it was going to happen and they wanted to know what to expect. Then when the final blow came…their parents told them they were getting divorced….I was often the one they told first. Why? Well, I guess it was because they realized they were now a part of my club. The divorced kids club, that is, and they wanted to know how I survived.

One thing I quickly realized was that no matter how different our backgrounds were or how different the parent's reasons for getting divorced were, the advice I gave my friends was always the same. It was the tips and tricks I'd learned over the last twelve years that helped me survive and find a 'new normal' that I was sharing with them.

1 IN THE BEGINNING

I'll never forget the day my parents told my sister and I that they were going to get a divorce. I was six and she was four. We all sat on the couch in the family room and my mom told us that she and dad were going to get a divorce and dad was going to live in a new apartment two towns away. She told me they both still loved us very much. Next she told me that we would spend some time with dad and some time with her. I immediately started crying.

Surprisingly, my sister didn't get upset at all. She was actually excited to go see dad's new apartment. Years later she would tell us that she really didn't have any idea what 'divorce' was and thought it has something to do with getting a new front door. She even went to preschool the next day and excitedly told her friends and teachers that her parents were getting a divorce, like it was something new and great. Well, you just can't make this stuff up. This is just the beginning of a crazy road you will travel. However, that said, life is a crazy road, and it's really what you make of it.

I hope that in the following chapters I can share some of my experiences and things I have learned that will make this book your go-to survival guide for tips and tricks that will help you get over the bumps in the road more easily, as they come your way.

2 CHANGE IS GOOD

I think there are very few situations where a kid does not have any idea that their parents are having problems. More than likely you saw your parents arguing about something on a number of occasions and you knew they weren't happy. Maybe you used your parents phone and saw a text or picture that gave you a clue there was something going on.

Many times, when parents are fighting, you might secretly hope that they do not get divorced, as you know it will change the only world you have ever known and the unknown can seem very scary. That is a typical feeling anyone would have. The reality is that divorce does happen, and the good news is that you can get through it and be just fine.

Through the many stories friends have shared with me, I have found that people find out that their parents are getting divorced in many different ways. Some parents handle telling the kids well and some parents don't. The *final event* that finally makes them decide to get the divorce usually has a big impact on how you find out that the divorce is moving forward. No matter how you get the information, the one thing that is for sure is that it begins a chain of events and big changes in your life and the life of others around you. So many more people than just your immediate family are impacted.

For you, one big change may be that, depending on the reason for the break up, you may feel sorrier for one parent or the other. The thing you have to remember, and this is a hard one, is that your parents are both going through major changes and crisis too. The life that they have been living for as long as they have been married is about to change. Your family's entire world has been turned upside down. Up until now you have only known one way of doing things, whether it has been your family's daily routines, regular activities or holiday traditions, just to name a few. A great deal of that will now change or maybe I should say, be altered.

Maybe you are thinking that change is bad? Well, if you really think about it, my guess is things have not been that great up until now. Maybe your parents have been fighting a lot and have been really upset. Whether it's been your parents fighting, not talking to each other, or some other sort of situation that made them unhappy with each other, this unhappiness and stress often trickles down to the kids one way or another. So, one way to look at it is that this new divorce will bring change to that bad or stressful situation.

Now I'm not saying that everything is going to be rosy and perfect. Again, life is hard and has many challenges, but what you can be sure of is that the bad situation that you or your parents have been living with will change. It's really going to be up to them and to you, to make it better, and communication and organization is the key to success.

The most important thing to do is to realize that divorce is a hard thing to go through, but as you continue to read through this book, I'm going to show you how you can survive.

■■

Here's where you can jot down some notes to help you walk through what might be swirling in your head...

- Take a minute to think about what has already changed since you found out your parents were going to divorce?

- Next think about what other things might change for you in the near future?

- What was hard before the divorce that has actually gotten better?

3 WHY ME?

So you may be thinking why me? Why did 'my' parents have to get divorced? Is it something I did? One thing I can tell you is that your parent's divorce is most likely not your fault. After all, you're the child and they're the parents!

Parents get divorced for so many reasons. In every divorce there's *his side and her side and the rest of the story*. What does that really mean? The reality is that nobody is perfect, and as much as we love our parents, they make mistakes too. Sometimes those mistakes can be what causes the divorce. Other times it's just that our parents had different ideas about what being married was going to be like. They may have had different ideas of what they wanted in life, or over time, they may grow apart and change.

I realize this is a really simplistic description of why parents get divorced. There have been hundreds of books written on the subject and every talk show host has talked about it and analyzed it!

The reality is that every situation is different, but the one thing that is the same is that it is not you that is the reason for the divorce. It's your parents. That alone should make you feel a 'little' better.

Read on....

✓ So here's where you give yourself a pass, and remember, you are not to blame for your parents' divorce. Unfortunately, you're just a casualty in the situation. Here's how to make the most of it...

4 BUILD A SUPPORT NETWORK

In order to get through life we all need a strong support network. My number one suggestion is that you build your support network of friends and family that you can trust and who care about you. One would hope that both of your parents can be a support for you, but depending on how each one is handling the divorce crisis may determine just how much they can or can't be there to support you now, or in the future.

The important thing is that you talk about your feelings and ask the questions you have. Bottling them up is not healthy and can be stressful. It's important to take care of yourself.

One thing you'll find is that kids of divorced families have to take on a lot more responsibility, because instead of two parents managing the house, now there is only one parent in each house. The 'parent team' that you once had has now dissolved and each parent is operating on their own. Before the divorce your dad may have handled all of the bills and was responsible for fixing things that broke, while your mom did all of the cooking and grocery shopping. There's a lot of things that need to get done to keep a house running. Now, instead of having two parents to take care of all of the chores and tasks, there's only one in the house, and now there are two houses to complicate things even further.

The more you can help each of your parents, the better. Even if it's just taking on the responsibility of taking out the garbage, cleaning out the dishwasher or making sure your room is cleaned up. Little things like this will really help the situation, as your parents will feel like they have a little help and they will not be as overwhelmed.

So back to helping you. If your family can afford it, then going to see a counselor can be a big help. A counselor is an objective person (someone who is not directly involved in the situation), who can give you an honest opinion. The advantage of a counselor is that they are not involved with all of the emotion and drama that might be going on. They can be the person that you can share your thoughts with and they're trained to help you in these situations.

A free option that might be available to you from one of your parent's companies is called an Employee Assistance Program (EAP). The EAP is a confidential, around-the-clock service that helps employees and their families balance the demands of work, life and personal issues like divorce. It provides support and resources for parenting issues, work-related situations, relationship problems, substance abuse or even self-improvement, and so much more. This confidential, employer-paid program is usually available to employees and others in the employee's household free of charge (that means you)! The EAP usually has a website and a toll-free phone number that employees and family members of employees can access or call. The EAP site my mom had access to had many different articles and checklists on divorce, moving, childcare, legal issues and more. When she needed new childcare for us, they researched different childcare centers in our area that she could look into. It was great, because it saved her time by having the EAP do the research, which meant she had more time for us and doing all of the new things she was taking on as a divorced parent.

When you call the EAP toll-free number you will reach very helpful representatives who are knowledgeable in almost any area you can think of! When you call, they will ask you what your question or issue is and then they can match you with someone that can start by helping you on the phone. It is completely confidential, so you can feel comfortable sharing information with them.

Some days it can be tough to manage everything that's going on and all of the change in your life. If you need help with something that is becoming a little hard to handle, or you find yourself in a crisis situation, your parents EAP can help you or them! Often from your parent's EAP program, they will offer three free counseling sessions in your area. Either way, EAP is a great resource when you or your family is going through change and a difficult time. If your parent is not sure if their company has an EAP program, they can ask their human resource benefits department.

All that said, counseling can be expensive and often when your parents are going through a divorce, a lot of money may be spent on lawyers and splitting up the things they own. This is where your school counselor can be very helpful. Hopefully they are someone you like and can feel comfortable talking to. The odds are you are not the first person that has gone to them with divorce worries! For all you know, their parents might be divorced and they know exactly how you feel.

If you are not comfortable with your school counselor, your school may also have a psychiatrist that is there part or full time that they can have you speak with. Usually your counselor, principal or a teacher can help you get an appointment with the school psychiatrist, or you can slip a note under his or her door and ask if they have some time to talk to you, and leave them your cell or email address. The number one thing is to go and talk to someone at your school that you trust. It could even be a favorite teacher from a previous year.

✓   It's important to talk out your feelings and ask questions about things that you're wondering about. No one is born knowing how to get through a divorce, but there are many people out there who are trained and can help you. Give it a try. I am sure it will make you feel better and if you're not thrilled with the first person you speak with, find someone else. It's all about finding the right match for you and your situation.

■■

Jot some notes or just take some mental notes here...

- What things will change now that you have just one parent in each house? Think how the responsibilities used to be split. You might have not even noticed, because what your mom did and what you dad did was all you knew...With the divorce, how will that change?

- Who's in your support network? Who else can you add?

5 JOURNALING

Another option that can be really helpful is to keep a journal. If you feel like all of the things that are going on in your life are spinning in your head and it's hard to stop thinking about them, then keeping a journal can be a huge help.

A journal can be many different things. First, it can be something as simple as a spiral notebook where you write down what is going on in your life and how you are feeling. If you are creative, you might want to start with a blank covered journal and draw pictures or glue things you love to it, to make it special.

Another option is to keep an electronic journal that you can access online from anywhere. This definitely helps so you can write in it, no matter whose house you are at.

One option is to use google documents to keep your journal. (Another nice thing about an online journal is that you do not have to worry about hiding it from your nosy brother or sister!)

If you are worried about what to write in your journal, simply start each entry with 'Today I….' and complete the sentence. Remember, this is your special place! Put anything good or bad in your journal. There's no right or wrong.

Remember, grammar and punctuation do not matter! You can even just write a few words that describe how you're feeling, or if you like to draw, add pictures or make it a comic strip.

Just getting your thoughts on paper is a stress reliever. If you write them down, then you can tell yourself that you don't have to think about them as much. Yes, I know that may be easier said than done, but writing down your thought of the day will really help you, because over time you will see that things that seemed horrible at one point got better.

If there's something in particular that is stressing you out, write it down and then read it out loud to yourself. After you read it, take in a big, deep breath, and then hold your breath for a count of three seconds and then blow your deep breadth out. As you are blowing it out, think that all of the things you just read that are bothering you are being released and are moving away from you across the room. I realize this takes a little bit of imagination. This is a trick that I learned in a yoga class I took. It sounds crazy, but it really worked for me!

Getting your thoughts written down is similar to sharing your thoughts with a counselor. Just getting it out of your head is a release. Give it a try. Remember, it's not a homework assignment. There is no right or wrong way to journal.

✓ Journaling is something that is all yours. Who knows, maybe someday you will write a book of all the things you learned while going through your parent's divorce that will help other kids in the way I hope I am helping you.

6 DON'T HIDE YOUR FEELINGS

When your parents get divorced it may seem like you are all alone, but the truth is that you are far from being alone. A key to getting through divorce is sharing how you really feel. Don't bottle up all of your feelings but instead you can talk to any number of the people I suggested in the 'Build A Support Network' chapter.

It's important to remember that other people have gotten through this and have been able to overcome being a child of divorced parents. I know that when your parents are divorced you feel like you are the only one who has parents that are not married, but the truth is that a lot of other kids in your grade probably are going through similar things, but they just don't talk about it in the open.

A lot of kids who go through divorce often get depressed. Again, this may be one of the most stressful things that has happened to you, and you are learning how to deal with something no one taught you about.

■■

There's no time like the present to start sharing your feelings and thoughts...
- List the top three things you want your dad to know about how you're feeling about the divorce:

#1

#2

#3
- List the top three things you want you mom to know about how you're feeling about the divorce:

#1

#2

#3

7 DEFINITION OF A FAMILY

Up until now you've probably always thought of your family as the people who live in your house. Moving forward it will be a little different.

The reality is that just because people live under the same roof doesn't make them a family. Family is truly something much more. Family is people who love you, care about you, are there for you when you need them and want what is best for you.

Divorce can often cause mayhem in families. The extended family (Grandparents, Aunts, Uncles, Cousins, etc…) often don't know how to act, what to do, or what to say the first few times they see you once the divorce is underway or in place. I suppose that's understandable, especially if this is the first divorce in the family. They too, just like you, will have to adapt to the new situation.

So be prepared, as some may say nothing, because they don't know what to say and some may say something that's awkward. Hopefully they'll just let you know that they are there for you if you need someone to talk to.

Holidays are a time that can be a little awkward, at least in the beginning. You, or your parent's agreement, may decide where you'll be for the holidays. Holidays can be a bit hard in the beginning, as there may be traditions that you had that involved the one parent that is now missing from the event.

Of course it will be hard, but I can tell you that it will get easier. Unfortunately, I don't have the magic thing you can do to not feel the void of the other parent being there. I can tell you that you and the family that you are with, will create new traditions and often kids of divorce feel like they get extra presents. Well, that's just one way to try and look on the bright side.

Some friends told me holidays were always stressful when their parents were together. Holidays can be stressful because of all of the pressures to buy gifts, cook, get dressed up and get together with family members they may or may not get along with well. If you had any of these issues between your parents, your holidays might be better than they used to be!

Well, the key to remember is that in the new divorced scenario, you will see over time that the definition of family is really the same. You might need to make some adjustments, but the only difference is that instead of being under the same roof, your parents are now located at different places. They still love you, care for you and want the best for you, just as much as they did before.

■■

- Jot some notes about how you think your family will change?

- What are you worried will be different related to your family? Who's the best person for you to talk to about this?

- Can you think of some things that might actually be better?

8 TWO DIFFERENT HOMES

There are a lot of challenges that having two different homes results in. Before the divorce, your parents probably divided and conquered the many daily and monthly tasks and responsibilities that take place with running a house and taking care of kids: grocery shopping, cooking, paying bills, taking out the garbage, cleaning the house, gardening, going to your games, teacher appointments and so much more. There are hundreds of things that have to be done. When they split, now they each have their own homes and have to each take care of all of these tasks. In addition, now there's double the cost, as there are two houses that have electric, water, taxes and all of the other costs that comes with managing a home. I can tell you that your parents will probably be stressed out with all of the new responsibilities they'll have to take on. Often they don't realize what the other one was doing until they have to do it!

When my parents first got divorced I was with my mom 60% of the time and with my dad 40% of the time. The schedule my parents decided on looked like this:

A 60/40 Schedule Example (60% of time with one parent, 40% of time with the other parent):

Mom's house every Monday, Tuesday and Thursday
Dad's house every Wednesday
Alternate houses every Friday, Saturday and Sunday night

The days outlined in the above schedule are just an example. It works nicely, because it gives each parent a few days with kids and then a few days off. Another nice thing about it is that every week, you get to see your parents. This helps them be involved with what's going on with you, your friends and school.

Do you think the 60/40 schedule would work for you? Are there certain days you need to be at one house versus the other? These are all things to consider.

After a number of years on the above schedule, my parents changed to a schedule where I am with them the same amount of time each year. I am with one parent 50% of the time, or half of the time, and with the other parent the other 50%, or half of the time.

A 50/50 Schedule Example:

- Mom's house every Monday and Tuesday night
- Dad's house every Wednesday and Thursday night
- Alternate houses every Friday, Saturday and Sunday night

The thing I like about each of the above schedules is that I get to see both of my parents during each school week. It helps them stay up on what is going on and it gives them some consistent days on and off from having kids.

There are many different kinds of arrangements parents will come up with in their divorce agreement. Usually it depends on the job they have and the job's demands or maybe it's just who is better at doing the day in and day out parenting. Some people will be with their parents equal amounts of time and alternate weeks. Any kind of scenario you can dream up can happen.

My dad moved into a new house with less bedrooms and that meant my sister and I had to share a room when we were at dad's. My dad bought us a bunk bed and that was very exciting, because I'd always wanted a bunk bed. I chose the top because I thought it was cool to be up and away from everything in my own little world. All that said, living in the same room with my sister was not always great.

In the beginning I kept most of my clothes at my mom's house, because I was there most of the time. Over time, however, I slowly moved more things to dad's house too. The reality is that having two homes, you will have to have duplicates of things at both houses. For example, each house will have to have a toothbrush, hair dryer, brushes, pajamas, towels, alarm clock….

Where you used to have just one set of something, now you'll have a set at moms and a set at dads. In the beginning, you can try and bring things back and forth, but it becomes a hassle to have to pack things up, and it's even harder to get things from one house to another if your parents are not dropping you off at the other's house at the end of the weekend. If for example, your dad's bringing you to school Monday morning and your mom's picking you up from school at the end of day on Monday.

Often the things that have to go between houses, I would pack up Sunday night in a duffle bag at dad's and he would leave it by the back porch at mom's after dropping me at school. This way it would be there for me when I got home. Another option is that your school might let your parent leave the bag in an office so he doesn't have to go by your house. The thing that is important is that you ask your teacher or principal if something like this can work. Remember, you are probably not the first person who has had this situation.

✓ My suggestion here is that you get a good-sized bag that is just yours to use as you go back and forth between houses. It helps you know where the things you move back and forth are, and it's easy to identify at either parents house, so it's harder for it to get misplaced.

■■■

Things to think about…

- How does the schedule your parents have agreed to work for you with:
  o Your school schedule?
  o Your sports / activities schedule?
  o Getting together with friends?
  o Getting homework done?
  o Other?

- What are things that you'll need to have at both houses?

- What will you need to carry back and forth?

16

9 LISTS

One super easy way to make sure you stay organized is to make lists. Lists help because you can plan out what you need at each house. It also helps so you will rarely forget something that you need at the other parent's house. Trust me, realizing you forgot something is the worst feeling ever and the hassle of having to go back after you are all settled in at one house is a pain!

Making lists is a quick and easy way to make sure you don't have do deal with forgetting something. I keep little note pads and pens placed around my room so when I think of something I'm going to need to bring when I move to my second house, I write it down on a post-it note and stick it on my door or mirror.

Another option, if you have a cell phone, is to use the feature that is often called 'Notes', 'List' or 'Tasks'. If you are like me, and you are rarely without your cell phone, then when you think of something you want to remember to bring with you, just put it on your cell phone list. When you are ready to pack for the move from mom's to dad's house, all you have to do is look at that one list for everything you want to bring.

I'd be lost without my lists and I definitely know I would not get as much done as I do. Having a list is also a great stress-reliever. When the item is on my list, I don't have to think about it or worry about it anymore. I know that when it comes time to moving houses, all I have to do is look at my list and I'll know everything I need.

10 FRIENDS

So once it's official, if you haven't already told them, you will want to tell your friends that your parents are getting divorced. Maybe it comes up because they're going to pick you up for a sleepover, or want you to go to their house after school and you have to ask a parent before you can go. No matter what the situation, telling friends that your parents are getting divorced may seem awkward and something you don't look forward to doing.

The reality is, it's nothing for you to be embarrassed about. It's not something you did, it's between your parents. Yes, your life is going to change as a result of the divorce, but your good friends are the ones that will be there for you. You'll find your good friends are the ones that will listen when you need someone to talk to or a shoulder to lean on.

If nothing else, this experience will help you find out who your real friends are. The friends that listen and are there for you and support you, you'll find, are your real friends. After all, this may be the first real tough situation you've ever had to go through in your life. Unfortunately, it probably will be the first of many, as life is made up of many ups and downs. It's important to remember that the experiences we go through and what we learn from each experience is what makes us the person we become.

The reality is that many marriages end in divorce today. It's sad but true. Everywhere we look people are getting divorced from celebrities to our neighbors.

✓ All I am saying here is that you're not alone, and there are many good friends out there that can help you through this difficult time.

11 SHARING INFORMATION WITH YOUR PARENTS

Being from a divorced family, you definitely have a lot more to deal with than most kids that just stay at one home. It's up to you to bridge the gap of information between your parents. I know this sounds like a lot of work and may seem unfair that you have to take on this responsibility, because it's your parents who got divorced.

The reality is that helping your parents get the information they need to be informed will make for a much better situation for everyone. When it comes to managing your school activities, sports and schoolwork there are a number of things you can do to help both parents know what is going on and make your (and their) situation easier.

When your parents were together, you might have sat down at dinner together and talked about your day at school as a family. Both parents were informed at one time, knew what was going on and would be there for you. You may have come home to your at-home mom and filled her in about your day and then she filled your dad in on what was going on, where you needed help, or when the next school play you were in was going to be. I know it is so annoying to have to repeat yourself twice and listen to your sibling's stories more than once, but both of your parents care about you and want to be a part of your life. That's a good thing!

When your parents are divorced, the common ground and sharing of information between your parents often stops. You might find that your parents are often upset with one another and might hold information from the other, or they may be too busy juggling and managing all of the new responsibilities they did not have before.

For example, if you had an at-home parent, now they might have to go back to work and the family sit-down meals are not as frequent or organized. I remember my mom picking us up from the childcare my sister and I went to after school. Because she had to go through a lot of traffic, she was often there at the last minute. As soon as we got home and in the door, she was putting the water up for pasta before she even had a chance to take her coat off! It was already 6:30 p.m. or later, we had to eat, finish homework, get help from her on questions we needed answered, and often more.

There is also a chance that you will have someone else taking care of you, whether it's a new childcare, a new babysitter or nanny in your life. Learning their rules and including another person in your circle is certainly more to deal with. I like to look on the bright side and think of it as one more person to help with all of the things that need to get done to manage a family.

✓   So remember, the more you help to share information and bridge the gap between your parents, the easier things will be for everyone. Divorce can be a difficult time, but by helping keep both of your parents informed with what's going on, you'll be helping make things so much easier for everyone.

12 SUCCEEDING IN SCHOOL

The best place to start with communicating to your parents about what is going on at school is with your teacher. She or he can be a huge help, as I will bet you are not the first student they have had that was from a divorced family! They might even be able to give you tips on things that they can do to help you share the information they pass out with both of your parents.

Start by making sure your teacher and school knows your parents are divorced. Next you will want to make sure they have both of your parent's email addresses and cell phones, so both parents will receive all of the alerts that get sent out.

Next there's the parent / teacher conferences that your school probably has one or two times a year. Depending on how well your parents are getting along, they may be willing to go to the parent/teacher conference together. If they really do not get along well, I know a lot of teachers are willing to hold two separate appointments: one with each parent. In addition, always ask that teachers can send your school report cards and any notes to both addresses. This way you're not the go between for your parents, and each of your parents will not get upset if the other one didn't inform them about something. You simply have to ask the teacher or school to make sure both parents emails and/or home addresses get copies of things or have your parents might have to request it.

If your school publishes a student directory in print or online, it is best to have both of your parents contact information in it, if the school can accommodate both sets of information. Most can list both and will...and if it's in print, make sure both houses have a copy of it. It will help your parents know whom to contact for what, or how to get in touch with your friends or your friends' parents.

Letting others know of your situation is important, especially teachers and your school. They know that divorce happens and it is hard on the kids as well as the family. As a result, they have a lot of things set up to make sharing information about you, your schoolwork and activities a lot easier.

✓ Let teachers and others at your school help! I'm sure they've been through plenty of these situations and might even have some tips for you!

✓ Make sure both parents are copied on all information about you:

- your grades
- school events
- sports information: practice, games…
- parent meetings

13 CALENDAR: KEEPING TRACK

There are so many appointments, events, practices and more that you and your parents need to keep track of. Now that you will be moving back and forth between houses, one good way to keep all informed is to use Gmail's calendar. Gmail's easy to use calendar feature is free and easy to access from any computer, tablet that is online or from a smart phone. Having a common online calendar is a great way for you and your family to keep track of important dates and events and does not require your parents to talk to each other, if it seems like they always wind up in an argument or stressful.

After setting up the calendar online from your computer, one of the first things you must put on the calendar is when you will be at your mom's and when you will be at your dad's house. It is a huge help to have this information in one place that is easy to access. It helps you have one go-to place to find out where you will be for a certain time period.

On the calendar mark the days you will be with each parent so you'll easily be able to access where you on a certain date. This really helps when you get an invite to a party. All you have to do is look at your calendar to know what house you'll be at. Then you can ask that parent if you can go. In my situation, whichever parent's house I was staying at, that parent made the decision and bought the gift if I needed one.

Here are some other important items to add to your calendar, in addition to the dates that you will be with your mom or your dad.

- Add important school dates from your school's calendar. Make special note of teacher holidays and school vacations, as these are dates that your parents might not have off from work and you will need to figure out what you will do on these days.
- Add activities such as play practice, clubs you need to attend.
- Sports or instrument practice is also a must for the calendar, especially if it is located at a place where you will need a ride there and then need to be picked up.

- If there are any unique days that your parents have worked out for you to be with one parent or another, you can add each unique event separately to the calendar too. For example, a parent's birthday or mother's or father's day. Also, you may switch holidays (Christmas, Thanksgiving, Easter, Hanukah, etc…) from year to year, so it is nice to have it on the calendar so you all in the know with who is where and when!

After you have added all of the dates that you know at this time, you will see there is a feature in the Google calendar where you can 'share' your calendar. You will want to share your calendar with everyone in your family. This will let everyone see the events you put online. Depending on what preferences you choose in the calendar, you can let the other people you share the calendar with also add events and comments to it if you want. One important thing to note is that in order to use Google calendar, you and everyone you want to share it with will need a Gmail account. The best part is, it is free. Google is not the only one who offers a calendar like this, it's simply the one my family has used and it has worked for us.

It's really helpful to have this information in one place as it can be hard to remember. If you or your parents have a smart phone, it's really easy to access with the Google calendar with the Google app.

As you get new dates and information, simply add it to the calendar. It's automatically shared with everyone.

Keeping track of where you will be and when helps you and your family knows where you will be and what is going on when. The main goal is to have a one-stop place for all to go, from anywhere they are located. It allows everyone to be in the loop and helps communication. Whether you use gmail or some other email account and calendar, the important thing is that you keep the information stored in one, easy to access place, that you can get from any place.

✓ This way, whether you are at your moms or your dads, friends house or grandparents house, you always have access to it if you have an internet connection.

14 HOMEWORK: A MOVING TARGET

Having your own email account will help you send papers or projects you are working on between your two houses. I like having a gmail account, because they have a feature called google docs that has been really helpful to me. Google docs let's you create documents and spreadsheets and save them in the 'cloud'. This is great, because you can access them anywhere just by logging into your gmail account. Whether you are at your mom's or dad's or anywhere with an internet connection, you can get to the latest version of your document.

Next, ask your teacher if it's possible to get two copies of any textbooks that have to stay at home or if there's an online version you can access.

There will be times when the school only has one copy to give each student. When this happens, it's up to you to make sure you pack the book in your bag, so it moves with you from house to house when you need it. Another option is that there are sites such as amazon.com that sell new and used textbooks. Just make sure you have the right edition if you order it online.

I'm going to keep this chapter short, as you really need to figure out what works best for you…and I really don't like talking about homework! YUCH! Who does..Your teachers are a great help here. Talk to them. It really makes a difference.

15 CAUGHT IN THE MIDDLE

Getting caught in the middle of your parents might have been something that happened before they were divorced, so you may already know it's not an easy thing. As parents go through being separated and then divorced, kids often get caught in the middle of their parents even more.

The reason for this, of course, is because they are not happy with one another so they try to avoid each other. Your parents may know that when they talk to each other, it often winds up in an argument or some form of stress for them. So, they will often use you as their 'go-between'. That means they use you as the person that can deliver the information to the other parent, whether it's on the phone, email, text or when you see them.

For your parents, it makes sense to use you to share information with the other parent because they see you as the one who can 'carry' the information to the other parent, without them being involved.

Parents often don't realize how hard that can be on you! Why? Well, when there's a lot of stress during the divorce, (you may already know that) they're not always thinking clearly. You may find that just bringing up any information about the other parent causes the parent you're with to get upset. So, you need to tell your parent that they need to find a way to communicate the information to the other parent. Your time with your parent should be filled with telling them all of the things that are going on in your life with friends, school and any activities you do. Of course, if there are things bothering you about the divorce you need to bring those things up too.

Something that happens a lot is that either or both of your parents might complain to you about the other parent. No matter how you feel about the divorce, it's hard to hear your parent say mean things, complain or just be upset about the other parent. The thing is, your parent is doing this because they are angry or hurt and they really just need someone to vent to.

If you hear a parent talking about the other parent, the best thing to do is to ask them to please not talk about the other parent in front of you or directly to you, because it creates a lot of stress for you. You can also suggest they use their Employee Assistance Program (EAP) if they have one. Sometimes they have so much going on that they forget that they also need to reach out and get help for all of the new things that are going on in their life.

✓ So remember, don't take part in your parents' arguments, fights or squabbles. Let them know they need to deal with each other or talk to someone that can help them with the things they are upset about. Not you.

16 TWO SETS OF RULES: DEALING WITH DIFFERENT PARENTING STYLES

When you lived under one roof with both parents, the rules you had to follow were usually a combination of what your mom felt was important and what your dad felt was important. If your parents disagreed on what a rule should be, they usually worked it out between them and then let you know what the rule was going to be.

The rules I am referring to can be with regard to anything. It might be something as simple as whether or not you have to make your bed every morning, what time you have to go to bed, or whether or not you have to go to church. Some parents want the house always cleaned up, while other parents just are not as neat or organized, and are fine with some things laying around.

When you were in one house, you were following what I call the meshed rules. Those are the rules that result from both of your parents' individual rules. Depending on which parent might have had the stronger personality, well that might have been the rule or rules you had to follow.

Now that your parents are divorced, they are each running their own houses and more than likely you will have a different set of rules in each house. This can often be hard on kids at first, but over time you really just get used to it. The best way to think of it is that when you go to different places you have different rules. It takes some time to get used to the new rules your parents will give you to in their home.

✓ If you have one rule that works well for you at one parent's house, share it with your parent. You never know, they may be willing to alter their rule to make it easier on you.

CONCLUSION: IT'S GONNA BE OK

So that's an overview of some of the key things you will deal with. Of course there are so many more. This book could never cover every issue that will come your way, as then it would be never-ending!

I hope that some of the points in here will help you, or more importantly, help you see that you're not alone and as many other kids have gone through a lot of the things you're going through.

The important thing to realize is that things will be OK. Many, many kids have survived their parents' divorce and you will too...and though it may seem impossible to believe right now, in the long, you will have many skills that other non-divorced kids won't have at your age.

You'll be a great project manager, because you will learn how to keep track of your things in different places. You'll see your parents' get new friends and that will let you meet different people you might not have met if your parents were still together.

If you move from house to house (or apartment to apartment), you'll have different rooms and things you might not of experienced. Give the changes a chance as fighting against them only makes it harder on you. If you're not happy, talk to your friends, family or someone at school that can help, and take some of the ideas from this book. They are meant to help you the way they helped me.

You will survive your parents' divorce and I promise you will be a stronger, more mature person in the long run. Maybe someday you'll write a book to help others too. I hope so.

ABOUT THE AUTHORS

Samantha Smith and Alexa Smith's parents divorced when they were four and six years old, making them the first of their friends to be part of a divorced family. They quickly learned that their lives as they knew it would never be the same and their lives compared to their friend's would also be different. As they navigated elementary school and high school, they learned through trial and error, how to survive: two houses, two sets of rules and the many additional issues they had to face with two homes and divorced parents.

Over time, they became the 'go-to' divorce experts for their friends on topics like; kids and divorce, dealing with parents while they go through the divorce and after, and dealing with teachers, friends, family and more when divorce occurs. Their friends wanted to know what to expect, what to do and how to handle things. As they realized they were frequently giving the same advice, they decided to put their tips in an easy-to-read format and make it available for kids all over the world.

The Divorce Survival Guide For Kids was born.

Printed in the USA
CPSIA information can be obtained
at www.ICGtesting.com
LVHW020302101123
763578LV00010B/402